ST. PATRICK'S DAY
Jokes
and
Riddles
for Kids Ages 8-12

Edited by Emily McKeon

This Book Belongs to:

_____

_____

THANKS!

Thank you for your purchase. If you enjoyed this book, please consider dropping us a review by scanning the QR code. It takes only 5 seconds and helps small independent publishers like ours.

Scripto Love
PRESS

ST. PATRICK'S DAY JOKES & RIDDLES FOR KIDS 8-12

Spot illustrations: Creative Fabrica & Freepik.com

Contents

Introduction

Prepare for a little blarney with the *St. Patrick's Day Jokes and Riddles for Kids*! Jam-packed with festive jokes, riddles, and puns about all things St. Patrick's Day, this wee joke book is sure to make your little leprechauns laugh out loud with its pot of gold-worthy puns and witty one-liners.

Whether you're reading alone, or with others, these laugh-out-loud jokes will have you Dublin over with laughter!

1
Leprechaun Laughs

**Why did the leprechaun
go outside?**

To sit on his paddy-o'.

**What is a leprechaun's
favorite type of music?**

Sham-rock 'n' roll.

**When does a leprechaun
cross the street?**

When it turns green.

What did the leprechaun
say when the video
game ended?

"Game clover."

What's a leprechaun's
favorite cereal?

Lucky Charms.

What's the best position
for leprechauns to play on
a baseball team?

Shortstop.

**What do you call
a leprechaun with a
sore throat?**

A strep-rechaun.

**What instrument does
a showoff play on St.
Patrick's Day?**

Brag-pipes.

**How does a leprechaun
work out?**

By pushing his luck.

**What does a leprechaun
call a man wearing green?**

A green giant.

**Why do leprechauns
have pots o' gold?**

They like to "go" first-class.

**What's a leprechaun's
favorite kind of tree?**

An evergreen.

Knock, knock.

Who's there?

Warren.

Warren who?

Warren a green outfit on St. Patrick's Day?

What's a leprechaun's favorite dessert?

Strawberry shortcake.

How old are leprechauns?

So old that they can remember when rainbows were black and white.

Why did the leprechaun stand on the potato?

To keep from falling into the stew.

**What do you get when
two leprechauns have a
conversation?**

A lot of small talk.

**Why do leprechauns
dislike leftovers?**

They prefer left-clovers.

**Why do people wear
shamrocks on
St. Patrick's Day?**

Because real rocks
are too heavy.

**Why can't you borrow
money from a leprechaun?**

Because they're always a
little short.

**What do you call
a leprechaun's
vacation home?**

A lepre-condo.

**What did the
leprechaun put in the
vending machine?**

A lepre-coin.

**How did the leprechaun
go to the moon?**

In a sham-rocket.

**Why are leprechauns
so concerned about
global warming?**

They're really into
living green.

**How did the leprechaun
win the race?**

He took a shortcut.

Knock, knock.

Who's there?

Irish.

Irish who?

Irish you
a Happy
St. Patrick's Day!

What do you call environmentally conscious leprechauns?

Wee-cyclers.

What job did the leprechaun have at the restaurant?

He was the short-order cook.

What did the naughty leprechaun get for Christmas?

A pot of coal.

Why do leprechauns
hate running?

They'd rather jig than jog.

Why are so many
leprechauns gardeners?

Because they have
green thumbs.

Why are leprechauns hard
to get along with?

They are short-tempered.

What did the baby leprechaun find at the end of the rainbow?

A potty gold.

What do leprechauns barbecue on St. Patrick's Day?

Short ribs.

Why do leprechauns prefer dollar bills to coins?

Because they're green.

How do leprechauns celebrate St. Patrick's Day?

By holding a lepre-concert.

Why did the leprechaun climb over the rainbow?

To get to the other side.

What is a nuahcerpel?

Leprechaun spelled backward.

Knock, knock.

Who's there?

Erin.

Erin who?

Erin so fast, but I couldn't catch the leprechaun!

Why do leprechauns make great secretaries?

They're good at shorthand.

What did the leprechaun tell his neighbor on March 17?

"Irish you a Happy St. Patrick's Day!"

Where would you find a leprechaun baseball team?

In a little league.

**What happens when
a leprechaun falls into
the Irish Sea?**

He gets wet, of course!

**What do you call a
leprechaun who gets
sent to jail?**

A lepre-con.

**Why did the leprechaun
turn down a bowl of soup?**

Because he already had
a pot of gold.

**What type of sandwiches
should they serve on
St. Patrick's Day?**

Paddy melts.

**Who catches the
lepre-cons?**

An under-clover cop.

**Why do the Irish reduce,
reuse, and recycle?**

They believe in
green living.

**What did the giant say
to the leprechaun?**

"Look up!"

**What do you call a frog
that jumped into a
pot of gold?**

A leap-rechaun.

**What are the best shoes to
wear on St. Patrick's Day?**

Lepre-converse.

Knock, knock.

Who's there?

Pat.

Pat who?

Pat on your coat we're going to the St. Patty's Day parade.

**What did one leprechaun
say to the other?**

"Let's take an elfie."

**How do you know when
leprechauns are fighting?**

They give each other the
gold shoulder.

**Why aren't
leprechauns barbers?**

They just don't cut it.

**What would you get if
you crossed a leprechaun
with a frog?**

A little man having a
hopping good time.

**What do leprechauns drink
in the morning?**

Irish coffee.

**What do leprechauns put
on top of presents?**

Rainbows.

**What do you call a
leprechaun prank?**

A saint pat-trick.

**What's a leprechaun's
favorite vegetable?**

Green beans.

**Why did the leprechaun
pour Coke into his
bread mixer?**

He was trying to
make soda bread!

2

St. Paddy's Day Smiles

**What do ghosts drink
on St. Patrick's Day?**

BOOs.

**What would you get if
you crossed Christmas
with St. Patrick's Day?**

St. O'Claus.

**Who is St. Patrick's
favorite superhero?**

The Green Lantern.

Why did St. Patrick drive all the snakes out of Ireland?

It was too far to walk.

When does Valentine's Day come after St. Patrick's Day?

In the dictionary.

How do musicians show off to their crush on St. Patrick's Day?

By serenading them with brag-pipes.

**What should you say
to someone running a
St. Patty's Day marathon?**

"Irish you luck!"

**What would St. Patrick
order to drink at a
Chinese restaurant?**

Green tea.

**Why do frogs love
St. Patrick's Day?**

They're always
wearing green.

**Which dog breed should
you invite to your
St. Patrick's Day party?**

An Irish Setter.

**Mom, I met an Irish boy
on St. Patrick's Day.
"Oh, really?"**

"No, O'Reilly!"

**What's long and green and
only shows up once a year?**

The St. Patrick's Day parade.

Knock, knock.

Who's there?

Saint.

Saint who?

Saint no time for questions, open the door!

**What did St. Patrick
say to the snakes?**

He told them to hiss off.

**How do you pay for soft
drinks on St. Patty's Day?**

With soda bread.

**Why did St. Patrick
drive all the snakes
out of Ireland?**

Because snakes can't walk.

3
Dublin Over with Laughter

What did one Irish ghost say to the other?

"Top o' the moanin' to ya!"

What do you call a fake Irish diamond?

A shamrock.

How can you tell if an Irishman is having a good time?

He's Dublin over with laughter.

**What does Ireland have
more of than any
other country?**

Irishmen.

**What's Dwyane Johnson's
Irish nickname?**

The Sham-Rock.

**What is Irish and left
on the lawn?**

Paddy o' furniture.

How did the Irish Jig get started?

Too much water to drink and not enough restrooms.

Why can't Irish golfers ever end a game?

They refuse to leave the green.

What do you call a bad Irish dance?

A jig mistake.

**What did the Irish referee
say at the end of the
soccer match?**

"Game clover!"

**When is an Irish Potato
not an Irish Potato?**

When it's a French fry.

**What's the difference
between Irish wisdom
and Irish luck?**

One is clever.
The other is clover.

Knock, knock.

Who's there?

Aaron.

Aaron who?

Aaron go bragh and all that Irish talk.

4
Luck O' the Irish Jokes

**What do you get when
you cross a pillowcase
with a stone?**

A sham-rock.

**What does it mean when
you find a horseshoe?**

Some poor horse is
going barefoot.

**Why don't you iron
four-leaf clovers?**

Because you don't want
to press your luck.

**How can you spot a
jealous shamrock?**

It will be green with envy.

**What type of spells do
Irish witches cast?**

Lucky charms.

**How is a good friend like
a four-leaf clover?**

They are hard to find.

What do you bake for an Irish birthday party?

A paddy cake.

What do you get when you do the Irish Jig at McDonald's?

A shamrock shake.

What does it mean if you find a four-leaf clover?

That you have too much time on your hands.

What do you get when you cross poison ivy with a four-leaf clover?

A rash of good luck.

Where can you always find a shamrock?

In the dictionary.

What type of bow cannot be tied?

A rainbow.

Knock, knock.

Who's there?

Ireland.

Ireland who?

Ireland you money if you promise to pay me back.

5
Miss O' Lanious Jokes

What did the Irish potato say to his sweetheart?

"I only have eyes for you."

What do you call an Irish spider?

Paddy long legs.

Why does the River Shannon have so much money in it?

Because it has two banks.

What's the perfect St. Patty's Day breakfast?

Green eggs and ham.

What's an Irish baby's favorite song?

Patty Cake.

What's green and sings?

Elvis Parsley.

What's big and purple and lies next to Ireland?

Grape Britain.

Why do the Irish always answer a question with another question?

"I don't think we do, do we?"

What do Irishmen say when you tell them Bono is your favorite singer?

"You too?"

Knock, knock.

Who's there?

Irish.

Irish who?

Irish I'd find a lucky four-leaf clover!

4
St. Paddy's Puns

Irish you were here.

Let's have a shamrockin' good time tonight!

Irish you a happy St. Patrick's Day!

I'm a clover, not a fighter.

It's time to paddy like
the Irish do!

You're the cutest clover
in the patch.

It isn't over 'till it's clover.

You're the life of the paddy!

A best friend is like a
four-leaf clover: hard to
find and lucky to have.

You're my lucky charm.

You shamrock my world.

Irish you a whole pot of gold!

I'm not Irish,
but kiss me anyway.

Made in the USA
Las Vegas, NV
08 March 2023

68764751R00037